PSALM 91
The Secret Place

Jane S. Rogowski

Psalm 91

"He that dwelleth in the secret place of the Most High shall abide under the shadow of the Almighty. I will say of the Lord, He is my refuge and my fortress: my God; in him will I trust. Surely he shall deliver thee from the snare of the fowler, and from the noisome pestilence. He shall cover thee with his feathers, and under his wings shalt thou trust: his truth shall be thy shield and buckler. Thou shalt not be afraid for the terror by night; nor for the arrow that flieth by day; Nor for the pestilence that walketh in darkness; nor for the destruction that wasteth at noonday. A thousand shall fall at thy side, and ten thousand at thy right hand; but it shall not come nigh thee. Only with thine eyes shalt thou behold and see the reward of the wicked. Because thou hast made the Lord, which is my refuge, even the most High, thy habitation; There shall no evil befall thee, neither shall any plague come nigh thy dwelling. For he shall give his angels charge over thee, to keep thee in all thy ways. They shall bear thee up in their hands, lest thou dash thy foot against a stone. Thou shalt tread upon the lion and adder: the young lion and the dragon shalt thou trample under feet. Because he hath set his love upon me, therefore will I deliver him: I will set him on high, because he hath known my name. He shall call upon me, and I will answer him: I will be with him in trouble; I will deliver him, and honour him. With long life will I satisfy him, and shew him my salvation.

Introduction

I have read Psalm 91 and written things about it for many years, but early one morning the Lord woke me up with this psalm on my mind. I went into the living room and sat before the Lord and He began to bring to my mind scriptures and examples that I could apply to this psalm. I pray you will be encouraged to put your trust in God in these days in which we live.

"He that Dwelleth in the Secret Place of the Most High"

God is the Most High. There is none higher than Him. To dwell means to live, remain, stay, abide. God wants us to seek His face, come into His presence, and spend time alone with Him. In that secret place we find peace, protection, rest, acceptance, and answers to our prayers. No one else can come into that secret place. It is reserved for you and God alone. It is a place where you meet with God one on one. God is waiting for you to come to Him. He wants to fellowship with you. He wants to help you and protect you. He wants to show you great and mighty things that you don't know.

Jeremiah 33:3, "Call unto me, and I will answer thee, and shew thee great and mighty things, which thou knowest not."

Psalm 31:19-20, "Oh how great is thy goodness, which thou hast laid up for them that fear thee; which thou hast wrought for them that trust in thee before the sons of men! Thou shalt hide them in the secret of thy presence from the pride of man: thou shalt keep them secretly in a pavilion from the strife of tongues."

Isaiah 30:18, "But the Lord still waits for you to come to him so he can show you his love and compassion.

For the lord is a faithful God. Blessed are those who wait for him to help them."

God is telling us to make our communion with him a permanent dwelling place. You draw near to God and He will draw near to you. You will find Him if you seek Him with your whole heart. God will not force himself on you. If we don't spend time reading the scriptures and praying then how do we expect to have any direction for our life? He is waiting for us to come to Him. We tell the Lord we love Him, but we don't give Him our time. I have found when I put God first and spend time talking to Him and reading His Word, I get so much more done and the day goes smoother. When I get too busy and put other things first, I don't accomplish everything I planned to finish that day. Many times, there are problems or interruptions that keep me from completing things I had planned to do.

John 15:4-5, "Abide in me, and I in you. As the branch cannot bear fruit of itself, except it abide in the vine; no more can ye, except ye abide in me. I am the vine, ye are the branches: He that abideth in me, and I in him, the same bringeth forth much fruit: for without me ye can do nothing."

Jesus wasn't talking about just enjoying occasional times of fellowship with Him. He was telling us to abide in Him. The word "abide" doesn't mean to go in and out; to pray and study your Bible and worship and praise the Lord one day and then ignore Him for days at a time or until the next service at church. That is not abiding. Jesus was a man of prayer. Even though He was the Son of God, He knew He had to spend quality time with the Father. Jesus prayed in the morning before daybreak. He prayed all night. He prayed in the desert. He prayed in the mountain. If it was important for Jesus to pray, it is important for us to pray.

The Bible says that Satan goes about as a roaring lion seeking whom he may devour. Don't let him devour you. Be on guard against him. If we don't spend time with God in prayer and the Word, we give Satan a chance to slip in and attack us and our loved ones.

I Peter 5:8, "Be sober, be vigilant; because your adversary the devil, as a roaring lion, walketh about, seeking whom he may devour."

The most important part of this psalm is abiding. If we abide or dwell in the secret place with Him, then we will abide under His shadow, under His protection.

A soldier would be severely punished if he walked away from his post for a few hours much less days at a time. While he was gone, the enemy could sneak in and harm or kill everyone inside the city. Satan is waiting for us to be off guard so he can slip in and hurt, destroy, or kill us and our loved ones.

St. John 10:10, "The thief cometh not but for to steal, and to kill, and to destroy: I am come that they might have life, and that they might have it more abundantly."

The people of God sometimes wonder why they have so much trouble and why things are not going well for them. Many times it is because they have neglected to pray and read the Word for days at a time thus letting the enemy in. God was trying to warn them, but they weren't listening. They were too busy doing other things. It may not have been things that were wrong, just things that kept them so busy that they had no time for God. A lot of things are fun, enjoyable, and even needful, but where does God fit into all of this?

The most important thing we can do is spend time with God. We are living in dangerous times and we cannot afford to squander our time on other things when our soul and the souls of our loved ones are at stake. Jesus told us that in the last days, dangerous or perilous times would come, and we are living in those last days.

When all these things begin to happen around us, we can say with the psalmist David, *"Thou art my hiding place; thou shalt preserve me from trouble; thou shalt compass me about with songs of deliverance"* (Psalms 32:7).

We need to be in union with the Lord. We can't be in union with Him if we love the ungodly things of this world. Don't feed on ungodly material off of the internet. That is how godly men have fallen. If you can't resist temptation, throw the computer in the trash. It is better to do that than to lose your soul. There is so much out there we don't need to be looking at. Those things that get into your eye gate and ear gate will eventually enter into your heart.

Matthew 15:19, "For out of the heart proceed evil thoughts, murders, adulteries, fornications, thefts, false witness, blasphemies."

Jesus said in St. John 14:15, *"If ye love me, keep my commandments."* Do we really love Jesus or do we love the world?

David said in Psalm 119:112-113, *"I have inclined mine heart to perform thy statutes always, even unto the end. I hate vain thoughts: but thy law I love."*

David was a man after God's own heart. He loved God and His Word and God blessed him with riches and honor. God will bless you with everything you need, want, and desire if you will fellowship with Him, love Him, and serve Him. As a parent, when my children were small and they would climb up onto my lap and hug me and kiss me and tell me they loved me, I wanted to love them back and give to them. God is the good Father and we are His children. When we love Him and spend time with Him, He wants to show His love for us by blessing us. There have been things I didn't have to buy because God blessed me with them. He has even given me things I liked but would not have bought for myself. It let me know that God was thinking about me and wanted to show me that He loved me. He wants to do the same for all of His children.

Psalm 37:3-4, "Trust in the Lord, and do good; so shalt thou dwell in the land, and verily thou shalt be fed. Delight thyself also in the Lord; and he shall give thee the desires of thine heart."

Psalm 84:11, "For the Lord God is a sun and shield: the Lord will give grace and glory: no good thing will he withhold from them that walk uprightly."

Psalm 145:19, "He will fulfill the desire of them that fear him: he also will hear their cry, and will save them."

There is something we have to do first in order to receive the blessings from God. Jesus said in Matthew 6:33-34, *"But seek ye first the kingdom of God, and his righteousness: and all these things shall be added unto you. Take therefore no thought for tomorrow for the morrow shall take thought for the things of itself. Sufficient unto the day is the evil thereof."*

Jesus is saying not to worry about tomorrow but to seek God first and He will take care of all those things you are so worried about. Jesus said in verses 25-30 of the same chapter not to worry about what you are going to eat, or what you are going to drink, or what you are going to wear. God takes care of the fowls of the air and we are more important than they are to Him. We can't even add an inch to our growth or a minute to our life, so why are we worrying about these other things. You aren't going to accomplish anything by worrying. Trust God. He loves you more than you can imagine. He will take care of you. David said in Psalm 37:25, *"I have been young, and now am old: yet have I not seen the righteous forsaken, nor his seed begging bread."*

"Shall Abide Under the Shadow of the Almighty"

In order to stay or abide under someone's shadow, we have to be very close to them all the time. You must be constantly in their presence. That is the place where God can instruct you in your daily life and warn you when you are in danger. There are so many ways that God can speak to you whether it is in a still small voice, through His Word which is the Bible, through visions and dreams, prophecies, messages taught or preached, or through an impression in which you just know on the inside what God wants you to do.

When my grandmother was in her 80's, she was in the hospital. She had not been eating and she was dehydrated. She was very weak and didn't know where she was or who she was. I was going to visit her that day but visiting hours didn't start until 12:00. So I sat down to read my Bible. I read different translations of the Bible and that day I was reading the Living Bible. When I opened it, my eyes fell on two words: "Go now." I almost fell off my chair. The Lord said to me, "Read my Word to her and strengthen her inner man."

I got dressed and arrived at the hospital at about 11:00 and they let me in. Nobody else was there. I spent time reading the healing scriptures to her. She knew them all by heart and quoted them with me word for word as I read.

A little while later, the doctor came in and asked her questions and she didn't know her name, where she lived, her children's names or anything else. When he left, I continued to read the healing scriptures and she quoted them with me as I read. The next day she went home and she was fine.

That showed me that even though she was aging and her mind wasn't functioning correctly right then, her inner man, her spirit man on the inside, was strong, quick, and alive.

2 Corinthians 4:16, "For which cause we faint not, but though our outward man perish, yet the inward man is renewed day by day."

Our spirit man on the inside is renewed by the Word of God. We feed our natural man food to strengthen our physical body and we feed our spirit man the Word of God to strengthen our inner man.

God has all power. There is nothing too hard for Him. He can do all things. When we are in His presence, we are built up and strengthened.

Obedience to God is very important. We must spend time with Him on a consistent basis by reading and meditating on the scriptures and praying and listening for Him to speak to us.

You still have to go about your daily work, take care of your family, and do whatever ministry God has given you to do, but you can be praying when your mind is not in motion. For example, you can be praying when you are washing clothes, cleaning the basement or garage, ironing, dusting, cooking, washing the car, walking the dog, or cutting the grass.

The Bible says to pray without ceasing. Pray every day, don't give up. Stay in an attitude of prayer throughout the day. Talk to God about decisions you have to make. The more time we spend in prayer and the Word, the easier it is to recognize the Lord's voice. We can rest and not worry about the future because we know God has everything under control when we are abiding under His shadow.

Proverbs 3:5-6, "Trust in the Lord with all thine heart; and lean not unto thine own understanding. In all thy ways acknowledge him, and he shall direct thy paths."

Psalm 37:23, "The steps of a good man are ordered by the Lord: and he delighteth in his ways."

Psalm 32:8, "I will instruct thee and teach thee in the way which thou shalt go: I will guide thee with mine eye."

If we don't pray and study God's Word then we will make mistakes. Just because we are born again believers doesn't mean we will automatically make right decisions but when we spend time talking to God, studying His Word, and being led by the Holy Spirit, then we will make wise decisions. It will save us time and money, give us wisdom in dealing with other people, open doors that we never thought we could walk through, and give us peace in our mind.

If you will let the Lord guide your steps, He will lead you in the right way, in the best path for your life. The safest place we can be in is the center of God's will and we cannot get there if we do not spend time with Him.

It is important to let God direct your path because if you try to act on your own plan and ignore what God is saying to you, it may mean disaster, especially in these days in which we are living.

When God gives you a plan, it may not always look like the best plan. People won't always agree with what God has told you, but remember, you are the one God spoke to, not them.

God called Abram alone and blessed him. He didn't call his friends and family. He only spoke to Abram. What God told Abram to do looked foolish in the natural. God told him to take his wife and all he had and move to another place, but Abram did not even know where he was going. The people in Haran worshipped idols. When Abram said, "God told me" they probably said, "God who?"

Despite this, Abram obeyed. He took his wife and nephew, Lot, and all they had and left Haran. God blessed him and changed his name from Abram to Abraham and made him the father of many nations as He promised. Abraham is called the Father of faith.

"I Will Say of the Lord, He is My Refuge and My Fortress, My God, In Him Will I Trust"

I will say, what are you saying about the Lord? It says "He is" my refuge and my fortress. Not going to be, He is right now. God is our refuge and fortress; He protects us from danger and strengthens us against the attacks of the enemy. David loved the Lord. He trusted in Him and worshipped Him. He never said the Lord was "going" to be anything. He always said "He is" everything that I need (Psalm 23).

Psalm 18:1-3, "I will love thee, O Lord, my strength. The Lord is my rock, and my fortress, and my deliverer; my God, my strength, in whom I will trust, my buckler, and the horn of my salvation, and my high tower. I will call upon the Lord, who is worthy to be praised: so shall I be saved from my enemies."

Psalm 28:7, "The Lord is my strength and my shield; my heart trusted in him, and I am helped; therefore my heart greatly rejoiceth; and with my song will I praise him."

God loved David. He was a man after God's own heart. When he sinned, he was quick to repent. He didn't blame anyone else for his sin.

Psalm 32:5 "I acknowledge my sin unto thee, and mine iniquity have I not hid. I said, I will confess my transgressions unto the Lord; and thou forgavest the iniquity of my sin."

Even though at times David was going through terrible things in his life, and he wrote about them in many of the psalms, he always came back with praise for the Lord. God loves when we praise and worship Him.

Psalm 105:1-3, "O give thanks unto the Lord; call upon his name: make known his deeds among the people. Sing unto him, sing psalms unto him; talk ye of all his wonderful works. Glory ye in his holy name; let the heart of them rejoice that seek the Lord."

When God called David's son Solomon to build the temple, David said in I Chronicles 29, *"<u>Now I have prepared with all my might for the house of my God</u> the gold for things to be made of gold, and the silver for the things to be made of silver, and the brass for the things of brass, the iron for the things of iron, and wood for the things of wood,; onyx stones, and stones to be set, glistening stones, and of divers colours, and all manner of precious stones, and marble stones in abundance. Moreover, because <u>I have set my affection to the house of my God</u>, I have of mine own proper good, of gold and silver, which I have given to the* *house of my God, over and above all that I have prepared for the holy house."*

David not only gave huge amounts of expensive things for the building of God's house, but he also encouraged the leaders and people to give. He got involved with what God was doing. David loved God and he did everything he could to prove that love.

"Surely He Shall Deliver Thee from the Snare of the Fowler and the Noisome Pestilence"

It says "surely" he shall deliver thee. There is no doubt about it. Satan is the fowler. He sets snares and traps for us and hopes we will fall into them. We go along not expecting anything to happen and all of a sudden we are hit with something unexpected that we don't know how to handle. If we have been abiding in the secret place, God will show us how to handle it. He can give us peace in the midst of the storm.

The word "noisome" means foul smelling. For example, there can be some kind of chemical spill or something with a strong odor that can make you sick. God said he would deliver you.

"Pestilence" is a deadly, incurable, contagious, rapidly spreading disease. We have been hearing reports about that lately and we will see more as we approach the coming of the Lord. It tells us in Matthew 24: 7, *"For nation shall rise against nation, and kingdom against kingdom: and there shall be famines, and pestilences, and earthquakes, in diverse places."*

When you see these things happening you don't have to be afraid. Jesus said in St. John 14:27, *"Peace I leave with you, my peace I give unto you: not as the world giveth, give I unto you. Let not your heart be troubled, neither let it be afraid."*

Psalm 32:7, "Thou art my hiding place; thou shalt preserve me from trouble; thou shalt compass me about with songs of deliverance."

Isaiah 8:13-14, "Do not fear anything except the Lord Almighty, He will keep you safe."

Isaiah 41:10, "Fear thou not; for I am with thee: be not dismayed, for I am thy God: I will strengthen thee: yea, I will help thee; yea, I will uphold thee with the right hand of my righteousness."

"He Shall Cover Thee with His Feathers, and Under His Wings Shall Thou Trust"

Years ago my grandmother told me a story about a barn that caught on fire and the mother hen was in the barnyard with her chicks. When the fire was over some men went to check on the damage. They found the scorched body of a mother hen and when they moved her body her baby chicks were safe and sound underneath her wings.

When a mother hen covers her little chicks with her feathers, you can't even see they are there. No predator can find them. They are hidden from the enemy.

Regardless of what happens in our life when the storm is over, we will come out safe and sound because we are under the Lord's personal protection.

Matthew 7:24-27, "Therefore whosoever <u>heareth these sayings of mine and doeth them</u>, I will liken him unto a wise man, which built his house upon a rock: And the rain descended, and the floods came, and the winds blew, and beat upon that house; and it fell not: for it was founded upon a rock. And every one that <u>heareth these sayings of mine, and doeth them not</u>, shall be likened unto a foolish man, which built his house upon the sand: And the rain descended, and the floods *came, and the winds blew, and beat upon that house; and it fell: and great was the fall of it."*

Both men went through the storm, but the man who built his house on the rock, which is the Word of God, and did what it said, came out victorious. The other man heard the same Word, but he didn't do what it said, and everything he had was washed away.

Psalm 24:19, "Many are the afflictions of the righteous: but the Lord delivereth him out of them all."

Let me tell you that many are the afflictions of the unrighteous, but they are not going to be delivered unless they repent and ask God to help them, and do what the wise man did.

God loves the human race so much that He gave His Son Jesus to die on a cruel cross so we could be saved from sin and have eternal life in heaven. Jesus, the spotless Lamb of God, was willing to come and pay the price for our sins. Now, we have to receive Him into our heart by faith.

John 3:16-17, "For God so loved the world, that he gave his only begotten Son, that whosoever believeth in him should not perish, but have everlasting life. For God sent not his Son into the world to condemn the world; but that the world through him might be saved."

Romans 10:9, That if thou shalt confess with thy mouth the Lord Jesus, and shalt believe in thine heart that God has raised him from the dead, thou shalt be saved,

II Corinthians 5:17, Therefore if any man be in Christ, he is a new creature: old things are passed away; behold, all things are become new."

"His Truth Shall Be Thy Shield and Buckler"

His truth, His Word, shall be our protection from the enemy. Jesus said in St. John 17:17 when He was praying to His Father in heaven, *"Sanctify them through thy truth: thy word is truth."*

St. John 8:32, "And ye shall know the truth (the Word), and the truth will make you free."

The truth you know will make you free. If you don't read the Bible to know the truth, it can't help you. The shield of faith and the sword of the Spirit are part of the whole armor of God.

Ephesians 6:16-17, "Above all, taking the shield of faith, wherewith ye shall be able to quench all the fiery darts of the wicked. And take the helmet of salvation, and the sword of the Spirit, which is the word of God."

Romans 10:17, "So then faith cometh by hearing, and hearing by the word of God."

We need to put the scriptures in our heart so our faith will be strong. We can never take a vacation from God's Word.

Hebrews 11:1, "Now faith is the substance of things hoped for, the evidence of things not seen."

You can't see the answer with your natural eyes, but you believe what God says in His Word. Keep believing until the answer comes. Never give up.

Hebrews 10:35-36, "Cast not away your confidence, which hath great recompense of reward. For ye have need of patience, that after ye have done the will of God, ye might receive the promise."

Ephesians 6:13-14 says when you have done all to stand, stand. Keep on standing. The answer is on the way. Habakkuk 2:4, Romans 1:17, Galatians 3:11, and Hebrews 10:38 says that the just shall live by faith. Faith is believing what God says in His Word as truth and that it will come to pass as He said only if we will believe and not give up.

Hebrews 11:6, "But without faith it is impossible to please him, for he that cometh to God must believe that he is, and that he is a rewarder of them that diligently seek him."

Until Jesus comes, we are going to have to use faith and patience. When we hold on to the Word, it changes our circumstances. Faith has to be in two places: your heart and your mouth. You must believe in your heart and say it with your mouth.

Romans 10:8, "But what saith it? The word is nigh thee, even in thy mouth, and in thy heart: that is, the word of faith, which we preach."

Deuteronomy 30:14, "But the word is very nigh unto thee, in thy mouth, and in thy heart, that thou mayest do it."

God told Joshua the formula for success. It's not hard but we just have to take the time to do it.

Joshua 1:8, "This book of the law shall not depart out of thy mouth; but thou shalt meditate therein day and night, that thou mayest observe to do according to all that is written therein: for then thou shalt make thy way prosperous and then thou shalt have good success."

Speak the Word, meditate on the Word, do what the Word says, and then you will make your way prosperous and you will have good success.

"Thou Shalt Not Be Afraid for the Terror by Night, Nor for the Arrow that Flieth by Day, Nor for the Destruction that Wasteth at Noonday"

God doesn't want us to be afraid. This is not a suggestion, it is a command. He would never tell us to do anything that would be too hard to do. Problems like sickness, financial difficulties, losing your job, going through a divorce, your children getting into trouble can make you fearful. Sometimes it may feel like Satan is literally breathing down your neck and telling you that you aren't going to make it and that you are going to die or lose everything you have. There may be gangs running around in your neighborhood shooting out windows and slashing tires or a hurricane may be on the way to tear down your house and all of a sudden thou shalt not be afraid isn't as easy as it sounded when there were no storms going on in your life. How can you keep from being afraid with so much bad news going on around you?

Philippians 4:6-8, "Be careful for nothing; but in everything by prayer and supplication with thanksgiving let your requests be made known unto God. And the peace of God which passeth all understanding, shall keep your hearts and minds through Christ Jesus. Finally, brethren, whatsoever things are true, whatsoever things are honest, whatsoever things are just, whatsoever things are pure, whatsoever things are of good report; if there be any virtue, and if there be any praise, think on these things."

The apostle Paul said to "Be careful for nothing." That means do not worry about anything, do not fret, and do not be anxious. We can choose what we think about. We can either dwell on the circumstances or dwell on the Word of God. We have to cast down those thoughts that are contrary to God's Word. Satan will bring fearful thoughts across your mind all day long if you will let him. We have to meditate on God's Word instead of the lies of the devil.

Fear is a spirit. If Satan can keep you afraid, he can defeat you. The joy of the Lord is your strength. Fear will tear you down but faith will build you up. You can't have faith and fear at the same time.

When fear tries to attack our minds we have to resist it in the name of Jesus. Say, "Fear, I resist you in the name of Jesus. Leave my presence now. I refuse to fear. God has not given me the spirit of fear but of power and of love and of a sound mind" (2 Timothy 1:7).

You may have to resist fear and quote the scriptures a hundred times a day at first, but after awhile you will have to do it less and less. Satan is not going to stay around very long if you keep hitting him with the sword of the spirit, which is the Word of God. He will always come back to try to bring that fear on you, but keep resisting him and quoting those scriptures and it won't take long to get rid of him. People say they resist Satan by using the scriptures but it doesn't work. Somebody isn't telling the truth because Jesus said to resist Satan and he would flee. If Jesus said it, then he has to flee but we have to be diligent. Jesus showed us how to resist Satan in the fourth chapter of Matthew. Every time Satan brought a temptation to Jesus, He said, "It is written", and He quoted the scriptures to him and Satan had to leave. Follow the example of Jesus and you will always get the victory.

2 Corinthians 10:3-5, "For though we walk in the flesh, we do not war after the flesh: (For the weapons of our warfare are not carnal, but mighty through God to the pulling down of strong holds;) Casting down imaginations, and every high thing that exalteth itself against the knowledge of God, and bringing into captivity every thought to the obedience of Christ."

Our weapons are not natural weapons, they are supernatural weapons. We have the name of Jesus, the name that is above every name; we have the whole armor of God so that we can stand against the wiles of the devil; we have the blood of Jesus because the Word says we overcome by the blood of the Lamb and the Word of our testimony; we have the Word of God which is sharper than any two-edged sword; we have the Holy Spirit because Jesus said that we would receive power after the Holy Ghost Spirit is come upon us, and we have the angels of the Lord that camp around about us. Wherever we go, they are with us. We do not have to be afraid.

Psalm 27:1, "The Lord is my light and my salvation; whom shall I fear? The Lord is the strength of my life; of whom shall I be afraid?"

Psalm 118:6, "The Lord is on my side, I will not fear: what can man do unto me?"

Proverbs 3:24, "When thou liest down, thou shalt not be afraid: yea, thou shalt lie down and thy sleep shall be sweet."

2 Timothy 1:7, "For God hath not given us the spirit of fear; but of power, and of love, and of a sound mind."

Proverbs 3:25-26, "Be not afraid of sudden fear, neither of the desolation of the wicked, when it cometh. For the Lord shall be thy confidence, and shall keep thy foot from being taken."

"A Thousand Shall Fall at Thy Side and Ten Thousand at Thy Right Hand But It Shall Not Come Nigh Thee"

This could mean in time of war or because of a plague or some other reason. There may be people dying all around you, but God said it would not come near you as long as we are dwelling in the secret place close to the Lord.

A dear friend of ours that has now gone home to be with the Lord told us that she taught her son Psalm 91 when he was a little boy. When he was in World War II and men were being killed all around him, he kept quoting this psalm. He came home safe and sound without a scratch. He believed it was because he kept God's Word in his heart and mouth at all times.

When she told me this, I decided to teach Psalm 91 to our sons. That was over thirty years ago and they still remember it today. I told them to meditate on this psalm often because there is so much going on around us today. We have God's promise of protection.

The children of Israel were slaves in Egypt and when they left, there were over two million people. They traveled until they came to the Red Sea. Pharaoh was sorry that he had let them go and he went after them with his soldiers and chariots. The children of

Israel had the Red Sea in front of them and Pharaoh and his army behind them.

God told Moses to hold out his staff over the sea. When he did the waters parted and they walked across on dry ground. When they were on the other side, the Egyptian army started to cross, but when they were in the middle of the sea God rolled those waters back and the wheels came off of their chariots and they all drowned. Thousands of Egyptians died but the children of Israel were safe on the other side.

Then Moses and the children of Israel sang unto the Lord. *"I will sing unto the Lord, for he hath triumphed gloriously: the horse and his rider hath he thrown into the sea. The Lord is my strength and my song, and he is become my salvation: he is my God, and I will prepare him an habitation; my father's God, and I will exalt him" (Exodus 15:1-2).*

If God could bring the children of Israel out of trouble, then He can bring you out of trouble. He is the same yesterday, today, and forever.

Isaiah 41:10, "Fear thou not; for I am with thee: be not dismayed; for I am thy God; I will strengthen thee; yea, I will help thee; yea, I will uphold thee with the right hand of my righteousness."

Psalm 124:8, "Our help is in the name of the Lord, who made heaven and earth."

Proverbs 18:10, "The name of the Lord is a strong tower: the righteous run into it and are safe."

Psalm 138:7, "Though I walk in the midst of trouble, thou wilt revive me: thou shalt stretch forth thy hand against the wrath of my enemies, and they right hand shall save me."

"Only With Thine Eyes Shall Thou Behold and See the Reward of the Wicked"

You will see the destruction of the wicked, but you will not be a part of it.

When the children of Israel were in Egypt, God sent plagues on the Egyptians but the children of Israel were safe.

When the city of Jericho was destroyed, Rahab and her family were spared.

Joshua told the children of Israel in Joshua 24:15 to choose whether they were going to serve the false gods or the true God of heaven. He said, *"But as for me and my house, we will serve the Lord"*.

God said in Deuteronomy 30:19, *"I call heaven and earth to record this day against you, that I have set before you life and death, blessing and cursing: therefore choose life, that both thou and thy seed may live."*

God has given us a choice, to choose good or evil. Your choice will affect future generations. God said to choose life. It is your choice. If you choose the way of sin, death, and destruction, then you will bear the consequences. Choose life, choose to serve the Lord, choose what is right. Turn your back on sin.

Psalm 145:20, "The Lord preserveth all them that love him: but all the wicked shall be destroyed."

Proverbs 11:8, "The righteous is delivered out of trouble, and the wicked cometh in his stead."

Proverbs 15:6, "In the house of the righteous is much treasure, but in the revenues of the wicked is trouble."

"Because Thou Hast Made the Lord, Which is Thy Refuge, Even the Most High Thy Habitation No Evil Will Befall Thee Neither Shall Any Plague Come Nigh Thy Dwelling"

God said no evil would fall on those that are dwelling in the secret place of the Most High and that no plague, which is an epidemic disease that claims the lives of many, would come near their dwelling.

When we love the Lord, cleave to Him, hold Him tight, and won't let go, then He will deliver us. No evil will befall us that we can't overcome. God has His hand on our life. David loved the Lord and desired His presence more than anything else in His life.

David said in Psalm 42:1-2, *"As the hart panteth after the water brooks, so panteth my soul after thee, O God. My soul thirsteth for God, for the living God: when shall I come and appear before God?"*

Psalm 63:1, "O God, thou art my God; early will I seek thee: my soul thirsteth for thee, my flesh longeth for thee in a dry and thirsty land, where no water is; To see thy power and thy glory, so as I have seen thee in the sanctuary."

David said he would not fear regardless of what went on around him. He said God was his refuge and strength, his place of safety. He looked to God in the time of trouble and he wasn't disappointed. Is that our testimony today?

Psalm 46:1-3, "God is our refuge and strength, a very present help in trouble. Therefore will not we fear, though the earth be removed, and though the mountains be carried into the midst of the sea; Though the waters thereof roar and be troubled, though the mountains shake with the swelling thereof."

Job went through a terrible trial. He lost everything he had and all his children were killed at one time. Then he got boils all over his body. His wife asked, "Why don't you curse God and die?" But Job never sinned with his mouth. He never said anything against God.

If God brought Job out then he can bring you out. It would be terrible to lose one child, but he lost all his children in one day. Everyone turned against Job, even his friends. He continued to trust God and in the end, God gave him back twice as much as he had before the trial when he prayed for his friends. His daughters were the most beautiful women in the land.

Psalm 37:39, "But the salvation of the righteous is of the Lord: he is their strength in the time of trouble."

Romans 8:38-39, "For I am persuaded, that neither death, nor live, nor angles, nor principalities, nor powers, nor things present, nor things to come, nor height, nor depth, nor any other creature, shall be able to separate us from the love of God, which is in Christ Jesus our Lord."

"For He Shall Give His Angels Charge Over Thee,
They Shall Keep Thee In All Thy Ways.
They Shall Bare Thee Up In Their Hands Lest Thou
Dash Thy Foot Against a Stone"

God sends the ministering spirits, the angels of the Lord to take care of us. Wherever we are, they are there with us at all times to watch over us and deliver us from trouble. We have personal body guards to watch over us day and night.

Hebrews 2:1, "Are they not all ministering spirits, sent forth to minister for them who shall be heirs of salvation?"

Psalm 34:7, "The angel of the Lord encampeth round about them that fear him, and delivereth them."

In 2 Kings 6:8-23, we read about Elisha and how the King of Syria sent his army with horses and chariots to capture him because he was telling the King of Israel all his plans. They came at night and surrounded the city of Dothan. When Elisha's servant went outside in the morning and saw the great army he said to him, *"Alas, my master! What shall we do? Elisha answered, Fear not, for they that be with us are more than they that be with them."*

Elisha's servant probably thought Elisha had lost his mind. All he could see was the two of them and a big army of horses and chariots surrounding the city. Elisha prayed, and said, "Lord, I pray thee open his eyes, that he may see". And the Lord opened the eyes of the young man; and he saw: and behold, the mountain was full of horses and chariots of fire round about Elisha. God had sent his mighty angels to protect Elisha.

Elisha prayed again and God smote the Syrian army with blindness. Elisha led them to Samaria, right into the enemy's hands.

Elisha prayed again and the Lord opened their eyes and they saw that they were in Samaria. Talk about a shock.

The King of Israel got so excited he said to Elisha, "My father, shall I smite them? Shall I smite them?" Elisha said, "Of course not, give them something to eat and drink and send them to their master. So they prepared a big feast and after they had eaten and drunk, he sent them away. The Syrians never again came into the land of Israel.

I'm sure there have been times when the angels of the Lord have moved danger out of our way and we didn't even know it. But there have been times when we knew there was no way we could have escaped harm without their presence.

Years ago my Uncle Joe was out in his driveway working on his big Buick car. He had it jacked up and he was lying under it. Some of you may remember those big cars with the long fins and fender skirts. The cars back then were big and heavy, not like the cars of today.

While he was under the car, the jack slipped and pinned him under the car. His wife was in the house with the windows closed and wouldn't hear him if he hollered for her, and he couldn't holler anyway because the car was lying on his chest. He knew if he laid there with that heavy car on his chest that he was going to have serious injuries, so with all his strength he lifted that big car off his chest and slid out. He knew he could not have done that in his own strength. He believed God had sent one of those big angels to help him. He did not suffer any injuries.

Psalm 103:20, "Bless the Lord, ye his angels, that excel in strength, that do his commandments, hearkening unto the voice of his word."

"Thou Shall Tread on the Lion and the Adder, the Young Lion Shalt Thou Trample Under Feet"

Jesus appointed 70 men to go into the cities where He would later come. He told them to preach and heal and they came back full of joy telling Him that even the devils were subject to them through His name. And He answered them saying, *"I beheld Satan as lightning fall from heaven. Behold, I give unto you power to tread on serpents and scorpions, and over all the power of the enemy: and nothing shall by any means hurt you"* (Luke 10:18-19).

It doesn't say Satan doesn't have power, but God has given us power over all of his power.

Jesus healed the sick, raised the dead, cleansed the lepers, and cast out devils. His disciples did the same thing He did and so did the Apostle Paul and the believers in the early church. Jesus said in St. John 14:12, *"Verily, verily, I say unto you, He that believeth on me, the works that I do shall he do also; and greater works than these shall he do, because I go unto my Father."*

When Jesus was on the earth, only those that were in the area where he dwelled were touched but now because He went back to heaven and sent the Holy Spirit to abide with those that have accepted

Jesus into their life, now people are being saved, healed, raised from the dead, and devils are being cast out all over the world.

Mark 16:15-18, "And he said unto them, Go ye into all the world, and preach the gospel to every creature. He that believeth and is baptized shall be saved; but he that believeth not shall be damned. And these signs shall follow them that believe; In my name shall they cast out devils, they shall speak with new tongues; They shall take up serpents; and if they drink any deadly thing, it shall not hurt them; they shall lay hands on the sick, and they shall recover."

The Word doesn't say these signs shall follow the preacher or the evangelist, but these signs shall follow those that believe. If we believe then these signs should follow us. Jesus Christ is the same yesterday, today, and forever. God never changes and His Word never changes. We should be seeing the same things happening today that we read about in the New Testament.

I John 4:4, "Ye are of God, little children, and have overcome them: because greater is he that is in you, than he that is in the world."

The greater one is living inside of every believer. He is greater than any disease. He is greater than any circumstances you will ever face. He said He would never leave you or forsake you but He would be with you until the end of the world.

"Because He Has Set His Love upon Me, Therefore Will I Deliver Him. I Will Set Him on High Because He Hath Known My Name"

When we love the Lord and continue to live for Him regardless of what we are going through, God will deliver us. We will rise above the cares of life because we know who He is and what He can do.

All of the God's promises are yours, but you have to receive them by faith and claim them as yours. They won't just happen because you read them. You have to meditate on those promises and thank God for the provision He has made for you through the blood of Jesus. Because of Jesus' blood, all of these blessings belong to the children of God.

He is Jehovah Rohi, our shepherd. He leads, directs and guides us in the way that we should go.

He is Jehovah Jireh, our provider. He supplies all of our needs according to His riches in glory by Christ Jesus.

He is Jehovah Shalom, our peace. He gives us peace that passes all understanding.

He is Jehovah Rapha, our healer. He sent His Word and healed us and delivered us from all destruction. Jesus bore 39 stripes on his back for the healing of our body and we accept it by faith in His Word.

He is Jehovah Tsidkenu, our righteousness. Jesus took our sin and gave us His righteousness. When God looks at us, He doesn't see our sin but He sees the blood of Jesus that washes away all of our sin.

He is Jehovah Nissi, our protector. God has all power and He has mighty angels that are at His disposal to move harm and danger out of our way.

He is Jehovah Shammah; He is always with us. He promised He would never leave us or forsake us, but that He would be with us until the end of the world.

He is Jehovah M'Kaddesh, our sanctifier. We have been delivered out of the kingdom of darkness, and translated into the kingdom of God's dear Son. We are set apart from sin's dominion and Jesus is our Lord.

He is El Shaddai, the God that is more than enough. He can do exceeding abundantly above all we ask or think (Ephesians 3:20).

"He Shall Call Upon Me and I Will Answer Him, I Will Be With Him In Trouble. I Will Deliver Him and Honor Him"

Are you in any kind of trouble today? God said for you to call and He will answer. He will deliver you out of trouble.

Psalm 34:17, "The righteous cry, and the Lord heareth, and delivereth them out of all their troubles."

Psalm 138:7, "Though I walk in the midst of trouble, thou wilt revive me: thou shalt stretch forth thine hand against the wrath of mine enemies, and thy right hand shall save me."

Psalm 50:14-15, "Offer unto God thanksgiving: and pay thy vows unto the Most High: And call upon me in the day of trouble: I will deliver thee, and thou shalt glorify me."

You will call, He will answer. It doesn't say we will not have any trouble. It says He will be with us in trouble and deliver us out of trouble. Everyone has some kind of trouble. You are not going to get through this life without ever having trouble. Jesus said, "In this world you shall have tribulation, but be of good cheer, for I have overcome the world." Jesus has overcome any trouble that we have to go through in this world. After He delivers you, then He honors you. It looks terrible while we are going through it, but knowing that God is with us, will deliver us, and bring us out with victory and honor gives us the strength and courage to continue to stand and not give up.

Jesus said he faced the cross with the joy that was set before Him. Why? Because He knew what the outcome would be: victory over Satan so you and I could have life and have it more abundantly; so we could be saved from our sin, overcome everything that comes against us, and spend eternity with Him in heaven.

Hebrews 12:2, "Looking unto Jesus the author and finisher of our faith; who <u>for the joy</u> that was set before him <u>endured the cross</u>, despising the shame, and is set down at the right hand of the throne of God."

We can have joy in the midst of trials and tests when we know what the outcome will be. We can know because we have all the promises in God's Word that promises us victory over Satan.

James 1:2-4, "My brethren, <u>count it all joy</u> when ye fall into divers temptations (trials, tests): <u>knowing this</u>, *that the trying of your faith worketh patience. But let patience have her perfect work, that ye may be <u>perfect and entire, wanting nothing.</u>"*

It says to count it all joy when you <u>fall into different trials and tests.</u> We don't plan trials and tests, they come our way unexpectedly. Some trials are worse than others. James says that the trying of our faith works patience. God doesn't bring the trials, but He delivers us out of them all. No one likes trials and tests, but if we will go through them with faith, patience, and integrity then we will come out with honor.

Shadrach, Meshach, and Abednego were promoted after the fiery furnace.

Daniel was made the most important man in the kingdom next to Pharaoh after the lion's den.

Joseph was made a ruler in Egypt after prison. He spent years in prison for something he didn't do but he continued to be faithful to God and be a man of integrity and he came out with honor.

Romans 5:3-5, "And not only so, but <u>we glory in tribulation</u> also: knowing that tribulation worketh patience; And patience, experience; and experience, hope: And hope maketh not ashamed; because the love *of God is shed abroad in our hearts by the Holy Ghost which is given unto us."*

Hebrews 6:12, "That ye be not slothful, but followers of them who through <u>faith and</u> <u>patience</u> inherited the promise."

Hebrews 6:15, "And so, after he had <u>patiently endured</u>, he obtained the promise."

Hebrews 10:36, "For ye have need of <u>patience</u>, that, after ye have done the will of God, ye might receive the promise."

Never give up, keep praying, believing God, speaking the Word, and waiting for your deliverance. You might as well be patient because there is nothing you can do about the situation. The more you gripe and complain, the longer you are going to stay in that situation. Begin to praise the Lord in the midst of that trial and you will come out a lot faster. Satan cannot stand when we praise the Lord.

Paul and Silas were put in jail for preaching the gospel. They were beaten and their feet were put in stocks. At midnight they prayed and sang praises to God and the prisoners all around them heard. Then suddenly there was a great earthquake, the foundations of the prison were shaken and all the doors were opened and every man's chains were loosed. The jailer woke up and saw all the doors open and thought the prisoners had escaped and he was going to kill himself. But Paul called out and told him not to harm himself because they were all there. The jailer went in and fell down before Paul and Silas and said, "Sirs, what must I do to be saved?" The jailer took them to his house and he and his whole family gave their heart to the Lord (Acts 16:19-34).

It wasn't easy for Paul and Silas to pray and sing praises to God when their backs were hurting and bleeding and their feet were in stocks. That is not a comfortable position to be in. We complain about a lot less than that. At midnight they began to pray and sing praises to God and it was loud enough that the other prisoners heard them. If Paul and Silas had sat in that prison and griped and complained, they would have been sitting there for a long time. However, when they began to pray and sing, God heard it and sent a big angel to shake the prison and bring them out. If we want to come out of trouble we have to praise the Lord.

Psalm 18:3, "I will call upon the Lord, who is worthy to be praised: so shall I be saved from my enemies."

"With Long Life Will I Satisfy Him and Show Him My Salvation"

That word "salvation" doesn't only mean forgiveness of sin, but it also means wholeness, soundness, safety, peace, healing, protection, deliverance, prosperity, and preservation. Everything you will ever need is included in this word "salvation".

God wants us to live out the number of our days in health so we can fulfill what He has for us to do.

Psalm 92:12-15, "The righteous shall flourish like a palm tree: he shall grow like a cedar in Lebanon. Those that be planted in the house of the Lord shall flourish in the courts of our God. They shall still bring forth fruit in old age; they shall be fat and flourishing; To shew that the Lord is upright; he is my rock, and there is no unrighteousness in him."

There are things that we must do in order to live a long life on this earth. We can shorten our life by the way we live. Some people live to be old, but they do not have a good, healthy, happy, prosperous life because they do not obey what God has told them in His Word.

Exodus 23:25, "And ye shall serve the Lord your God, and he shall bless thy bread, and thy water; and I will *take sickness away from the midst of thee. There shall nothing cast their young, nor be barren, in thy land; <u>the number of thy days I will fulfil</u>."*

Deuteronomy 5:33, "Ye shall walk in all the ways which the Lord God hath commanded you, that ye may live and that it may be well with you, and that ye may <u>prolong your days</u> in the land which ye shall possess."

God told us to honor our parents. There are special blessings to those that honor their parents. Whenever I see similar scriptures in the Old Testament and the New Testament, I take special notice to them.

Exodus 20:12, "Honour thy father and thy mother: <u>that thy days may be long</u> upon the land which the Lord thy God giveth thee."

Ephesians 6:1-3, "Children, obey your parents in the Lord: for this is right. Honour thy father and mother; which is the first commandment with promise; <u>That it may be well with thee</u>, <u>and thou mayest live long on the earth</u>."

It doesn't say to honor your father and mother if they deserve it, it says to honor your mother and father if you want things to go well and live a long life on this earth. There are parents that don't deserve honor because they have deserted their children or because of the things they have done to them, but out of respect and honor for God and His Word, we have to honor our parents. Don't let people keep you from the good things God has for you. Romans 5:5 tells us that the love of God has been shed abroad in our hearts by the Holy Ghost. If we have God's love in our heart then we can forgive. I know it isn't easy to do, but God will help you and He will bless you. When Job prayed for his friends then God healed him and gave him back double everything that Satan had stolen from him.

Psalm 34:12-14, "What man is he that desireth life, <u>and loveth many days</u>, that he may see good? Keep thy tongue from evil, and thy lips from speaking guile. Depart from evil, and do good; seek peace, and pursue it."

I Peter 3:10-11, "For he that will love life, and see good days, let him refrain his tongue from evil, and his lips that they speak no guile: Let him eschew evil, and do good; let him seek peace, and ensue it."

We have to be careful what we say about people and how we treat them if we want to live a long, good life. We grieve the Holy Spirit when we do not walk in love. The Holy Spirit is the one doing the work in the world today and if we grieve Him, then how do we expect to receive the blessings of the Lord and get our prayers answered?

Ephesians 4:29-32, "Let no corrupt communication proceed out of your mouth, but that which is good to the use of edifying, that it may minister grace unto the hearers. And grieve not the Holy Spirit of God, whereby ye are sealed unto the day of redemption. Let all bitterness, and wrath, and anger, and clamour, and evil speaking, be put away from you, with all malice; And be ye kind one to another, tenderhearted, forgiving one another, even as God for Christ's sake hath forgiven you."

Putting God's Word in our heart and keeping His commandments yields length of days, long life, and peace. When we say "commandments" we think of the Ten Commandments, but whatever God tells us to do in His Word is His commandment. Jesus said in St. John 14:23, *"If a man love me, he will keep my words: and my Father will love him, and we will come unto him, and make our abode with him."*

God said that whatever we ask, we would receive if we believe on the name of his Son Jesus Christ and love one another.

I John 3:22-23, "And whatsoever we ask, we receive of him, because we keep his commandments, and do those things that are pleasing in his sight. And this is his commandment, That we should <u>believe on the name of his Son Jesus Christ, and love one another</u>, as he gave us commandments."

Proverbs 3:1-2, "My son, forget not my law; but let thine heart keep my commandments; <u>For length of days, and long life</u>, and peace, shall they add to thee."

Even though we love the Lord and are trying to please Him, we miss the mark. We all miss it sometimes and need to ask forgiveness. God is ready, willing, and able to forgive us of our sin and to cleanse us from all unrighteousness.

I John 2:1-2, "My little children, these things write I unto you, that ye sin not. And if any man sin, we have an advocate with the Father, Jesus Christ the righteous: And he is the propitiation for our sins: and not for ours only, but also for the sins of the whole world."

God loves you so much that He sent His Son Jesus to die for your sins and mine. Jesus arose from the dead and sits at the right hand of God the Father making intercession for our sins. When we receive

Jesus as our Savior, He takes our sins and gives us His righteousness. Regardless of what you have done, when you repent, your sins are washed away by the blood of Jesus never to be remembered against you anymore. You become a new creature in Christ. Old things have passed away and all things are new.

If you have never received the Lord Jesus Christ as your personal Savior, you cannot abide in that secret place of the Most High that I have talked about in this book. Right now, you can receive Jesus into your heart and life and become a child of the Most High God. You can have a personal relationship with Him. If that is your desire, pray this prayer with me.

"Lord Jesus, thank you that you died on the cross to save me from my sin, and that you arose, and sit at the right hand of God making intercession for me. Please come into my heart and forgive me of my sin. I turn from sin and turn to God. I want to live for God from this day forward. Thank you for receiving me into your family. Please fill me with your Holy Spirit. Amen."

If you have prayed this prayer and you really meant it you are now a child of God and you belong to His family. Read your Bible and pray every day, get into a Bible believing church, fellowship with other believers and you will grow in the Lord.

73853417R00040